My Life, My Story
A Father's Legacy, A Buffalo Soldier's Journey

Henry F. Wright

With
Sheila Wright Stamm, PhD

Foreword by
Richard Stamm, JD

Text copyright © 2019 by Sheila W. Stamm

Photographs copyright © 2019 by Sheila W. Stamm

All rights reserved. No part of this publication may be reproduced or stored in a retrieval system or transmitted in any form or by any means, electronic, mechanical, photo-copying, recording or otherwise, without written permission of the publisher and the copyright owners.

First Edition with Minor Revision (July 2019).
978-1-7323670-1-2

To my father, who helped me become who I am and, more importantly, who I want to be.

Henry, Sheila, & Rich

Foreword

This book highlights the story of Henry Floyd Wright, a Korean War veteran born and raised in North Carolina who lived and lives his life standing up for what is right. Challenging a system rife with racial discrimination, he raised and educated three beautiful children who, in their own ways, followed similar paths – one of them is my wife. Fearless, she too lives her life standing up for what is right in a way that makes him proud. Although her story is barely mentioned here, she is nonetheless very similar to him—dry wit; funny; simultaneously strong, insightful, sensitive, caring, and compassionate; like him, she will fight for what is right, even when challenging the status quo is the most unpopular thing to do and comes at great personal/professional cost. Like him, she understands that there are interests greater than self-interest and causes nobler than self-advancement. This book is her way of honoring him; of saying "Thank you."

Besides the obvious influence of his family growing up, it was his experiences in the Korean War as a Buffalo Soldier that most shaped his worldview and life-long commitment to his fellow man. As a combat infantryman in the 17 day Battle of Chosin Reservoir – rightly called "The Most Harrowing Battle of the Korean War" – Henry learned an invaluable lesson. In the face of life-threatening cold (25°F below zero) and a surprise attack by 120,000 enemy soldiers that completely encircled the entire US force, in the face of inadequate food, warm clothing, ammunition, and cold-resistant equipment, Henry learned that in the heat of battle, men will look out for one another with a simple, unquestioning, sacrificial devotion stronger than the bonds of home or family. When he came home, he carried that lesson with him and lived his life by a code of honesty, integrity, personal responsibility, perseverance in the face of adversity, and an abiding desire to care for others, often anonymously and at his own expense. In that regard, he's always been true to who he is and never been ruled by what people thought he should or shouldn't do.

If, as Martin Luther King said, "Life's most urgent question is: what are you doing for others?," Henry has lived the answer.

-Richard Stamm, JD

His /Story

This is the life story of my father, who was born in the early 1930s to parents who deeply valued education, farmed, and owned land in eastern North Carolina. Key to his family is that they lived in what is now arguably one of the "poorest" counties in North Carolina. Yet, his parents (only one generation removed from slavery) educated their children and owned land even when most Black folk either did not or could not. Except for the brief period defining my youth, wherein the majority of us graduated from high school, went to college, and successfully entered professional positions with ease in the 60s, 70s, and 80s, nothing much has changed since my grandparents were alive. The good ole boys resurrected their altered states and re-enacted a mutated form of racialized consciousness on descendants who no longer recall or know their history.

Raised in a loving family together with his 3 sisters and 5 brothers, my father married his high school sweetheart (my mother) and within seemingly the blink of an eye became a loving husband, dedicated father of three, and Korean War veteran. As a soldier, he fought under the leadership of General Douglas MacArthur as a Buffalo Soldier in the 24th Infantry Regiment of the U.S. Army. Many now wonder how this is possible given that the Buffalo Soldiers were an all-Black infantry named for their bravery by the Native Americans shortly after the Civil War. Tracing its origin to July 1866, most are unaware that the 24th Infantry was active until 1951 and again from 1995-2006, however, the last group of fully segregated Buffalo Soldiers fought along with my father in Korea. Few recognize that Buffalo Soldiers fought bravely for the United States in a segregated 24th Infantry for over 85 years. This means that the Buffalo Soldiers in the segregated 24th Infantry served not only throughout the Western United States after the Civil War, but also fought bravely in every war from the Spanish-American War to Korea. It was not until after the Korean War that the last of the all-black units in the United States military was abolished in September 1954. As a Buffalo Soldier, my father's legacy as "brave" was reinforced and he continued to be brave in fighting for his Civil Rights once home.

In the years following Korea, my father re-enlisted and later worked as a civilian on an Army base in Fort Lee, Virginia. He retired from Fort Lee as Director of the Audio-Visual Division in the 1980s – after having fought consistently for his right to be appointed the position for which he had been previously repeatedly, systemically denied for a number of years on the basis of skin-tone. This story is his legacy and that of my own. Had he not fought for his rights and discrimination not overturned, I doubt very seriously if many others (myself included) would have gained access to positions previously held primarily for whites. Now, years later, I see a surge in similar practices and wonder how many young folk know and understood the magnitude of what people gave of themselves – often their very lives – just so a few could have equitable rights of many. Now, facing some of the same barriers faced by my father, albeit in mutated form, I am cognizant perhaps more than ever before of what my father and his peers went through to achieve the position.

My father's story (and indeed my own) is as much about our humanity as it is persistence in the face of adversity. Such dynamic is reflective of what life is like living in a nation/world so filled with promises too often denied. It is also about the many contradictions defining a person's legitimacy in the world as an "other." Such notions form the residual undercurrents that define one's inner heart. When not addressed, we see the mismeasure of man – not our higher selves. Instead, folk justify both action and inaction based largely on unexamined assumptions. The myriad of historical, political, and economic nuances that gave rise to these social constructs in the first place are meaningless without knowing what led to the arbitrary categorization of race and racialized isolation reflected in gendered, socio-cultural, and ethnic affiliations.

Still, I must clarify unequivocally that this is my father's tale of two lives – that of a soldier and that of a Black man living in a segregated, now mutated United of States divided by those who know and those who no longer remember. As such, it is his story, in his own words, as shared with me, his daughter and a reflection of my own. Together our story is my way of giving voice to his life so that his legacy might benefit others in their quest for even greater wisdom in our endless love for humanity and desire to uplift us all beyond the boundaries of trapped consciousness into a universe of possibilities.

-- Sheila

Henry & Gladys

My Life/My Legacy
Henry F. Wright

Chapter 1
Growing Up "Down South"

I was born on the third of July in 1931 to Katie Kee and James Walter Wright on a farm we sharecropped with Turner Stevenson near Garysburg, North Carolina. I was two years old when my father was told by Turner Stevenson that, since he kept such good records, he should have his own farm. My mother then rented a farm from Johnny "Doc" Buffalo adjoining my grandfather's where we lived until we built our own house on my mother's property in 1948.[1]

By renting and farming my mother's land, we were spared the discrimination and harsh treatment from the "white man." [Such treatment was typical for many who did not own land and share-cropped with white farmers in the southern region.]

My mother and father could read and write so they worked hard to see that all of their children received a high school education. Some of us received an education beyond this. My sister Doris went to school and became a registered nurse and my sister Katherine a practical nurse. My brother Roger was trained as a tailor, worked in this capacity, and owned a barber shop. My brother Al became a businessman with several stores and two buildings in New York. I was admitted to Virginia State University to receive training supportive of my ability to become the first African American civilian as a audio-visual director at Fort Lee, Virginia. I also received a license in residential wiring for electricians at a local community college and completed several advance training programs offered at the federal level.

---

[1] My father's grandfather was the son of a woman indigenous to the land now known as Virginia and a man from England who settled in Northeastern North Carolina.

Our children went even further than we did with their education. My brother Roger's daughter has a PhD in microbiology and two other daughters also attended college at Virginia Union. My sister Doris' daughter graduated from West Point and is a MD currently practicing in South Carolina. My sister Katherine's son graduated from Central University in Durham, North Carolina and I made sure that each of my children similarly went to college. My son attended A &T State University in Greensboro and each of my daughters have graduate and professional degrees—one is a JD licensed in intellectual property law and the other a PhD and former dean in higher education. Other nieces and nephews, including great nieces and nephews, also completed college. Some of the great nieces and nephews also received graduate and professional degrees.

Getting into Mischief
While growing up as a kid, I stayed in something all the time. One day, while my mother was washing, I fell into a tub full of water on my head. Fortunately, my mother grabbed me just in time to keep from drowning. There was also the time when I put my mother's belt around my neck for a necktie and left home. When I was missed, the family had to track me down. They could see my tracks because, in those days, we had dirt roads. My family finally found me after a frightful search. I guess that is why I have been going ever since.

I was the baby of the family for four years until my sister Doris was born. Her arrival gave me someone to play with and made three sisters in total: Doris, Katherine, and Esther.

Esther was the oldest and had to help mother cook. Every Saturday, she would bake cakes for Sunday's dinner. I would always wait for the cake bowl and chocolate bowl.

All of my brothers were older than me so I only had my sisters to play with.

School Days
When growing up, the next oldest child would have the responsibility of keeping the baby while everyone worked. I remember my first day of school. Katherine and Esther took me. I was five at the time so I had to wait for the next school year until I was six.

After starting school, I tried not to miss a day, even if I was ill. I was well liked by the teachers and, from the beginning, tried to be the best in the class. While in the first grade, the teacher, Mrs. Newsome, took me and Jack Buffalo home on the weekend. Her home was in Elizabeth City. We got to ride on the ferry because this was the only way to get to her home at the time. We had three teachers at the three-room school. There were two females and one male. The male was the principal of the school.

Teachers and parents had a good working relationship during those days. Parents would often visit the school to make sure their children were well-behaved.

As I reached the fifth grade, my brother Alfred had finished school a few years early and decided it was time for him to move on. So, he left for New York City and told me I would have to help my father on the farm. I still never missed a day in school because I would either go to school until Noon or work in the morning and go to school in the evening. Math was my favorite study because I got help from my sister "Kat" (Katherine).

In elementary school, there were no inside facilities. The boys had a separate toilet from the girls. The school was

---

[2]The reference to "war years" is specific in this case to World War II.

heated by stoves and, each morning, the fire had to be started. I was well trusted so the two female teachers gave me a key to the school in order for me to make fires so that everyone could ha a warm environment when they arrived at school. For this, I was given seventy-five cents, which amounted to $1.50 a month. This was during the war years[2] so I would put money in war bonds.[3]

I finished elementary school as salutatorian.[4]

High School
I entered high school in 1945. There were many good times while in high school. I played basketball and baseball, which were the only sports available to us at the time. We bought an old school bus with the back glass missing as an activity bus and painted it yellow and black (our school colors). During our last year of high school, we won every tournament and had many trophies.

Northampton County Training School (NCTS), where I attended, was the only high school with a gym available for us to play in. The gym was built by students who preceded me in school. You could see daylight through cracks in the walls, but this didn't matter. All of the tournaments were also played in our gym because no other high school had one. This is why we had an advantage over the other teams and normally won.

[2] The reference to "war years" is specific in this case to World War II.

[3] "War bonds" were used in the US during WW I and WW II to finance military operations and are essentially government securities designed to increase in value for the owner.

[4] Salutatorian is the second highest rank in the graduating class.

My High School Graduation Photo

Our high school building was rather new, but it had to be heated by potbelly stoves, which burned coal. We had an outside toilet my first three years of school. In my junior year, the county finally put in steam heat along with indoor toilets, which were located under the school. Although technically, "indoor toilets," this meant that we still had to come outside to get to the toilet in the rain and snow.

Achieving the American Dream
After my brother Alfred left home for New York, the burden fell on me to help carry on the farm. year my father had given me a side crop, which was smaller than his own, and I assumed more and more responsibility. I began by planting a garden like that of my father's. By the time my brother Alfred left home, I had advanced to planting Spanish peanuts and it wasn't long before I was managing crops on my own.

I guess my father giving me responsibility on the farm helped make me into who I am today.

While working along with the rest of the family, I let them know that I intended to marry, but that I did not want my wife to have to work in the fields as my older brother did. I also wanted a car and house not knowing exactly how this was going to be accomplished. I was to work while my wife looked out for my children.[5]

[5]"Societal norms upheld for families at the time was that men worked and women stayed home to care for children. It was not until the 1970s and 80s that women received greater equity within the home and workforce.

I graduated from high school on the 18th of May in 1950 and, with nothing else to do, I started hanging with my classmates who were planning to enter the U.S. Air Force. They were riding around in a 1950 new Ford so I later decided to accompany them to the Air Force still not wanting to leave my high school sweetheart.

My buddies and I took the test for the U.S. Air Force in Raleigh and only two of us passed—me and my friend Robert Ruffin. The two of us were supposed to be sworn in and go to San Antonio, Texas to complete training. However, Robert had to travel back home to get his birth certificate. In the interim, I was left in Raleigh by myself and went over to Shaw University to visit a few friends. By the time Robert returned, I had enlisted in the Army and decided to go to Fort Knox along with other buddies from Rocky Mount.

Top Left: My Wife Gladys' Graduation
Bottom: Gladys, Me, and Friends

Chapter 2
Marrying the Girl of My Dreams

The first time I saw my high school sweetheart, she was getting off the bus in a green sweater. I felt immense joy and knew then she was going to be my wife. The night before leaving for Fort Knox I had already asked her parents for my wife's hand in marriage. I remember her mother telling her that she did not know how to treat a husband. My wife's reply was that she would treat me like her mother treated her Daddy. Both my wife's father and mother then agreed.

Gladys on our Wedding Day

I would finally marry the girl of my dreams. She later agreed that she knew we were meant for each other. It was hard leaving her to enter the military, but just knowing one day we would be united together gave me the initiative to go on.

I left my car, a 1941 Chevrolet, with my sister Esther. At the time I thought this was for safekeeping.

Basic Training
After being sworn in, I was shipped out to Fort Knox in Kentucky and began basic training. Many times, I asked myself if I was dreaming.

During basic training, I met two buddies—Robinson from South Carolina and Booth from Tennessee. While other boys went to town on the weekend we went to the movies on Saturday and Church on Sunday. I will never forget the song that the Chaplin sang each Sunday—Come Ye Disconsolate. The song gave me something to build on while being away from home and going through the miseries of basic training. The first two weeks in basic training was spent cleaning up the company area and setting out trees. We had to wait until we filled up all four barracks before starting the actual training. All of our officers and enlisted men that started in basic were black, but soon after President Truman started integrating the military services, which began in 1951.

We had barely been in basic one month when the war broke out in Korea. Now I knew I was in big trouble. I asked for and received permission for a leave of absence to come home and get married.

Saying "I Do"
I arrived home the second of July 1950 and was married in Emporia, Virginia by the Justice of Peace four days later on the sixth of July. After the ceremony we celebrated at home. All of my wife's friends came by to celebrate with us. It was the happiest time of my life.

With My Wife's Great Aunt.

On the eighth of July, reality set in that I had to return to Fort Knox. Up until now, married men were not allowed to enlist in the military, but by June 1950 this changed and men with families were being drafted.

Saying Goodbye
After returning to Fort Knox we learned that our basic training had been cut from 16 weeks to 8 weeks because of the shortage of men fighting the war in Korea.

On the first of September 1950, I received orders that I would be shipped out to Korea. I was given a 14-day delay in route home before continuing to Fort Lewis in Washington.

On the way home, I got my first taste of discrimination. Those of us on leave had stopped at a restaurant in Tennessee and was told we could not come in. Instead, they showed a hole in the rear of the building where we were to be served. After putting in our order, we waited until it came. They poked the food through the window, we took it, and (frustrated by it all) got back on the bus without paying. Here we were on our way to Korea to fight a war and was being treated like this.

I arrived home the second of September 1950 in time for Labor Day. My wife and I spent the day with my brother Alfred looking for Sea View Beach in Norfolk. It was dark when we finally found it only to find that it had been closed for years.

After spending a joyful 14 days together it was now time for us to part not knowing if we would ever see each other again. To ease the pain, I told my wife we were going to Fort Lewis Washington for more training.

The day I left, my mother in-law prepared me a big box of food, including a whole coconut cake.

Chapter 3
Korea Bound

We returned to Louisville to catch a train to Chicago. While in Louisville, we had a long wait so the white boys with us on the trip decided to go to a movie and all of us went with them. Once at the theatre we were told us that blacks could not enter. So, the white boys decided not to go in either and we all went to another theatre in town. This time we were wiser. The white boys bought enough tickets for each of us and we all entered the movie together. To my dismay, the picture playing that night was Rope of Sand, a movie I had seen in New York in the Summer of 1949. I was really relieved when the movie was over so that we could return to the train station.

Here we were on our way to Korea to help stem the flow of communism and to make sure that South Korea remained free. However, we had just encountered an experience at the movie theatre clearly demonstrating that we were not truly free at home.

The train finally arrived for Chicago where we were to meet troops for the train to Fort Lewis in Seattle, Washington. After arriving in Chicago some of the boys went to the movies, but I remained at the train station.

The troop train arrived and we loaded aboard. This was another new experience for me because we had to pull K.P. duty aboard the train. It took us over a week to arrive in Seattle. By the time we arrived, my friends and I had finished the cake my mother in-law made for me.

Fort Lewis and Pier 91
After arriving at Fort Lewis, Washington we were belittled by the tar paper shacks and pot belly stoves. The situation was made even less tolerable by having to pull guard duty at

night just in case one of the shacks caught fire.
We visited the service club at night where we got beer for fifty cents per pitcher. It seemed that everything was up hill.

We stayed at Fort Lewis for a few days before being transferred to the Port of Embarkation at Pier 91. Once at the Pier we turned in all of our belongings and was issued new clothing and equipment, including our weapons. While there everybody was in a rush to get us out to Korea because of the need for replacements for the men who had been killed and wounded. In the rush 18 of our records were lost.

We would meet in formation each morning and our names never came up. One morning, officers realized that we were still there and started to put us on K.P. duty in the large, consolidated mess halls. We had to prepare many bags of potatoes, but at least we had a potato peeler.

At first, we would go on K. P. and, after breakfast, keep on going out the door and to the Service Club. We would spend the entire day at the Service Club until the Mess Sargent finally became wise to us and started taking our Chow Pass when we came on K.P. duty.

We remained at Pier 91 during the heavyweight fight between Ezzard Charles and Jersey Joe Walcott. [6]

Leaving for Korea
On morning we lined up for formation and all of our 18 names were called to fall out for Korea. We had been at Pier 91 for almost two weeks. We finally finished processing and was shipped out to Korea on a four-engine airplane.

---

[6]"The fight between Ezzard Charles vs. Jersey Joe Walcott took place at the Yankee Stadium in New York on September 27, 1950. The fight was broadcast and heard in this case via radio, not TV.

We did not have jets in those days and it was a rough ride with all the air pockets and vibration on the aircraft. During our flight one of the plane's engines went out and we had to stop on a small island in the Pacific. There was only one woman on the island and that was the Post Commander's wife. It was very cold there because there were no trees and we remained there until a motor was flown out to replace the bad one. We were finally on our way to Japan where we arrived early in the morning. Japan was a complete wreck from the bombing of World War II.

In Japan we met soldiers who had been wounded and sent back to the hospital for treatment. Korea was so in need of personnel that they did not wait until soldiers' wounds had completely healed. We were told that many of our buddies that arrived before us had already been killed in action.

In Japan we were also taken to the rifle range to fire our weapons. Once we fired our weapons, we were then loaded on a ship bound for the coast of Korea.

Chapter 4
Buffalo Soldiers in Korea

We arrived in Korea early in the morning at Pusan. Upon arrival, we were unloaded from the ship and placed on trains that had been in battle and were shot up with blood all in them.

I will never forget what Korea looked like that morning. Trees had been bombed on the hills and were still smoking.

We were issued ammunition that morning and was on our way to the front lines. That night, while in route, the train suddenly stopped. You could hear all the bolts on rifles clicking. We did not know what to expect and, after being given the "all clear" signal we were on our way again.

Our next stop was the 24th Infantry Regiment Service Company where the 18 of us were placed on Security Guard for the next week. While there, we visited the morgue where all the bodies that had been blown apart were kept. This was a unique experience.

There was a young man named Young that was on guard with us every time it came time for his watch we would awake only to find him asleep.

We were finally loaded onto trucks and, this time, we stopped at Headquarters 2nd Battalion of the 24th Infantry. They were indeed glad to see us and immediately placed us on 24-hour guard at the Headquarters. This was our assignment. Although the Headquarters 2nd Battalion was not authorized as a security platoon, we remained there.

We were previously assigned to other companies before arriving at the 2nd Battalion. My assignment earlier was the "M" company in the 3rd Battalion, which was a heavy weapons company consisting of machine guns, mortars, and 57 Recoil ES rifles. At the 2nd Battalion, we were re-assigned to the 24th Infantry Regiment, which consisted of all black men otherwise known as Buffalo Soldiers. This was the last of September.

Buffalo Soldiers
The United States Congress authorized the creation of the 9th and 10th Calvary and the 38th and 41st Infantry regiments on July 28, 1866. In Spring of 1869, the 38th and 41st infantries were combined and became the 24th Infantry Regiment. The 39th and 40th became the 25th Infantry Regiment. These six regiments were organized with black men enlisted in the army staffed by white officers. Many were veterans of the Civil War.

Following the Civil War, two Cavalry and two Infantry regiments were sent to the western frontier of the U. S. to fight domestic wars with native American Indians. The soldiers were provided aged horses, deteriorating equipment, and inadequate supplies of ammunition. Yet, they performed admirably during this time for almost 20 years, participated in over 100 engagements, and were collectively awarded 18 Medals of Honor for their service.

According to the legend, native American Indians gave the troops the name Buffalo Soldiers given their bravery and fighting spirit, which reminded them of the buffalo. The soldiers accepted the name, which was offered as a term of respect and honor.

Similarly, during the Korean war, the 24th Infantry received the Republic of Korea Presidential Unit Citation for their service and was well-decorated with over 175 silver stars. Two members of the 24th Infantry also received the country's highest award, the Congressional Medal of Honor, offered by the U. S. Army. Once again, Buffalo Soldiers had demonstrated the character of bravery established earlier.

In March of 1944, the 9th and 10th Cavalry Regiments were deactivated in North Africa. The 25th Infantry Regiment followed and was deactivated in 1946. The 24th Infantry in which I fought was deactivated in Korea on October 1, 1951. This ended an era of segregated policies in the military and the 24th therefore became the last all black segregated regiment in the army.

On the Run
By the first of October 1950 we had the North Koreans on the run. Each day there was a notice placed on the bulletin board stating that the Red Chinese were massing on the Yalu River coming down to protect a power plant in that area.

As we pushed forward, we leap frogged with trucks. One group would walk while the others were trucked forward. Once the trucks unloaded, they would return to pick up others walking. This continued until we arrived close to the Yalu River. By then, it was November.

Thanksgiving dinner was served to the troops, but by the time we arrived off the hill from being on guard, all the turkey was gone. We had to eat eggs and bacon. While eating, we were told there was a gap in the "C" company line due to the loss of many men that previous night. We were ordered to move up in order to strengthen the line. This was my first night on the line and I can assure you it was not a joyful one.

Fighting raged all night. Some of the older soldiers reminded us that as long as you could hear the shells going over us, that we did not have to worry. They added that it was when you did not hear anything but an explosion that we had to worry.

Withdrawing from the Hill

We made it through the night and food finally arrived to us about 1:00 o'clock that afternoon. After lunch, we were told that the Chinese had us nearly surrounded and we were ordered to start withdrawing. We left off the hill and, once we were at the bottom, all eighteen of us loaded on the tanks with the notion that we were safe with them. When the tanks stopped for the night we were in for the surprise of our life. We had to guard those tanks with all our might.

The next day, we started walking. There were many roadblocks and we lost our trucks and jeep, including those belonging to the medics. If you got wounded, it was tough. The more we walked, the more surrounded we became.

One Sunday evening the bulldozer cut a trail across a mountain and marked it with engineering tape for us to follow at night. We pulled out at dark across the mountain and walked until the next morning. Some of the men became exhausted and, given that we had no vehicles, we had to leave them behind. It was all each individual could do to make it themselves.

It began to snow that night and, just before day, a few half truck vehicles came by. The Commander put every man of his own on the vehicles and told us, that if we were separated and all got out, where to meet. We tried to get on the half trucks but our energy was spent from walking across the mountain. We had to use our last strength to board those half trucks.

During the night the enemy was so close that the 159th Field Artillery had to fire point blank into them in order for us to slip through. We continued to walk all the next day and finally entered a small town where we thought we would get a break. We were immediately put on guard. Our luck lasted about two-hours when we had to pack up and continue to withdraw.

The Security Platoon was ordered to cover the battalion withdrawal and, when the last man was out, we were to follow.

When the last man had gone through, we prepared to follow when a white officer from one of the line companies pulled his gun on us and ordered us to remain in position. We quickly got him told that we were already put on orders and were not part of his company. After convincing him, we took our machine guns and moved out. That night we had a large obese white officer that could hardly make it tell us what he would do for us if we helped him out. We did and that was the last time I saw him. His name was Captain Kaiser.

That night we did not catch up with our company so we loaded up on ammunition trucks that were waiting to pull out. We waited until morning before they began to move. By that time, Chinese mortars were dropping everywhere. All we needed was for a mortar to hit one of those trucks loaded with ammo. So, we got off, caught up with some Quarter Master trucks, and loaded up on these instead.

That morning we discovered two of our buddies missing. Instead of remaining with us, they decided that they needed some rest. Rather than pull guard, they had elected to sneak out to sleep in some hay stacks. They wound up having to fight their way out with the line company that day. They finally caught up with our company two days later and swore that they would never pull another stunt like that again. Both had seen people dying all around them and one had a soldier shot in the head in the same fox hole with him.

Leadership Change and New Assignment
We walked from Thanksgiving until two weeks before Christmas before getting a break south of the Imjin River. The Chinese lines had grown longer and they had to trans-

port men and material all the way from China. This was just about impossible because of our Airforce planes and they were only able to walk at night. During this time, General McArthur was replaced by General Matthew B. Ridgeway.

The Battalion Commander was notified that the Security Platoon was not authorized and would have to be disbanded because of the need for replacement soldiers for those killed on the front line while withdrawing from North Korea. Myself and another boy from Washington, D. C. were asked if we would join the Intelligence and Recon Platoon. We quickly agreed and were given new assignments.

It had been two weeks since we had any resistance from the Chinese. Anticipating a Chinese attack on Christmas Day, orders were issued to serve troops Christmas dinner a day early. No one wanted to be caught celebrating.

After dinner on Christmas Eve, the Intelligence and Recon Platoon was given orders to cross the frozen Imjin River and search a town north of the river for any movement from the Chinese. We were to search the town that night and, if we did not contact the Chinese, ordered to pull back to a hill to set up an observation post. We were also ordered to stay at the post until we had contact with the enemy.

After crossing the Imjin River we came to the town we were to search, three of us, the Squad Leader Radioman and Assistant Radioman and I stayed outside of town while the remaining squad entered the town to begin the search. After about an hour we heard voices coming toward us on the road. We thought it was our men returning until they were about 20 feet from us. To our surprise, we were face-to-face with a Chinese Patrol. The element of surprise was the only thing that saved us. We withdrew under fire behind the embankment of the road until we were a safe distance from the Chinese. There we waited for the rest of our men to return.

While waiting, we heard small arms fire and believed that the rest of the squad had either been killed or captured. Meanwhile the squad searching the town was having their own problems.

Corporal Johnson had stopped a Korean on a bicycle and started questioning him when he looked up to see the Chinese army moving down the road. He immediately threw the Korean off the bike and started to withdraw when he discovered that they were between the patrol and the main body of the Chinese army. With the squad's fire power, they were able to escape, but thought that the three of us waiting outside of town had either been killed or captured. So, they withdrew back across the Imjin river to Headquarters and made their report.

Headquarters wasted no time calling in the Airforce night fighter planes to destroy the enemy. This created a problem for the three of us still in the area who had been waiting for the squad to link up with us.

The planes attacked us as well as the enemy, but we again were able to escape by hiding under a cement embankment under a railroad. We remained there until the next day, which was Christmas, before returning back across the Imjin River to Headquarters. We were met with a joyful return knowing that our mission had been accomplished and all men had returned safely.

We were later promised the Bronze Star for our actions that night. However, we were later told that we could not receive it because we did not have an officer present when the activity occurred. My wife had sent me a box for Christmas, but I was not able to eat or sleep for the next few days.

On New Year's Day we were again asked to return back across the Imjin River. This time we were accompanied by a Lieutenant Wright and three men from Fox Company. We tried to cross the river that night but did not succeed because the ice would break each time we tried. During the night, our radio was disabled so Sergeant Baker told Corporal Broussard and I to take the radio back to the 35th company and wait for them.

Sergeant Baker and others proceeded to cross the river. The Chinese had made it down to the river and was waiting for them to cross. When the last man crossed the river, the Chinese cut them off. They had to fight their way out with only receiving one man being wounded.

The group linked up with us at the 35th company where we had New Year's Day dinner, which consisted of frozen turkey. Company leaders asked why we were there and we told them we were on patrol. They then informed us that we were on our own because our unit had pulled out during the night. The Chinese had broken through the ROK line during the night. We left the 35th Regiment in search of our unit and caught up with some Quartermaster trucks loaded with food. We finally discovered our unit two days later.

The Last Push
We set up a line of defense South of Seoul, Korea south of the Han River. This was to be the last push by the Chinese, which had lasted from Thanksgiving until January. We held these positions until March 7, 1951 and began a push forward across the Han River North of Seoul. This was a day to remember. There was a tall hill to take after crossing the river. This was the first time that the Fox company lost most of their men and was the first time fighting without their regular commander Captain Waller who had left Korea for Japan. The hill changed hands numerous times before be-

ing secured by our troops. We took many prisoners that day.

The push lasted until April when again we were forced to withdraw back to Line Golden north of the Han River. This was to be our last offensive position and a position we held until October 1, 1951 when the 24th Infantry Regiment was deactivated. During those hard six months or more we were rotated home. I happened to have 13 months in active duty so I was in that number. We had survived weather 29 degrees below zero with inadequate clothing and equipment and thousands of Chinese.

My Wife & Son

Throughout this time, I carried what had now become a war-tattered photograph of my smiling wife with our new baby son in my wallet. I looked forward to coming home.

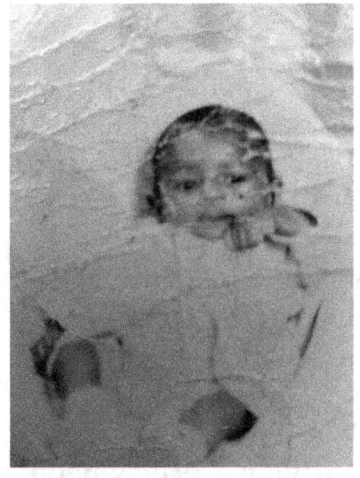

My Son Jerry

Chapter 5
Coming Home

After leaving the line, I was processed at the 25th Division Replacement Center, then back to Japan for further processing for the trip home by ship. After leaving Japan by ship we sailed for the next 13 days before coming into view of the Golden Gate bridge in California. I knew that I had finally made it back to the U.S.A. After processing in Richmond, California I was flown by plane back to Fort Jackson, South Carolina and then by bus to Roanoke Rapids, North Carolina. Once in Roanoke Rapids I hitched a ride to my wife's home with Freddie Puttney and entered a joyful reunion with my wife, son Jerry, and my in-laws. After this reunion I proceed down to my parents' home.

Once arriving home, I discovered that my car, the 1941 Chevrolet, that I left with my sister Esther for safekeeping had been picked up by my brother Alfred and taken back to New York. He was not working at the time.

The first week I was home, my brother Alfred and a friend of his had been to Kentucky and stopped by on their way back to New York. I questioned him about my car. Al told me that he sold the car and did not have the money, but if I would return with him to New York, he would stand up for me to get another one. They were driving a 1949 Ninety-Eight Oldsmobile. So, my wife and I traveled with them back to New York and we found a 1948 Fleet Line Chevrolet over in New Jersey. I made the down payment on it and my wife and I headed back to North Carolina.

After spending 30 days I was to report back to Fort Jackson for re-assignment. My wife and father-in-law went with me and came back on the bus from South Carolina.

Re-Assignment
After being processed I was assigned to Fort Eustis, Virginia.[7] After getting this, I found that there were no quarters for blacks so I immediately asked for a transfer to Fort Dix, New Jersey, which came through the 22nd day of February, 1952. This was George Washington's Birthday and it was on a weekend. The Post was deserted. I decided to take a chance and go to New York. On my way, I picked up another G.I. that took me into New York to Canal Street and gave me instructions on how to get to my brother's house. After spending the weekend there, I returned to camp.

I found a room in Bordentown, New Jersey with an old couple that owned two or three houses there. After getting the room, I returned to North Carolina and picked up my wife and son Jerry.

Discharge
We remained in Bordentown until my discharge in May 1953, which by then I had obtained the rank of Staff Ser-

---
[7] Fort Eustis in Virginia was later combined with Langley Airforce base.

geant. After returning back to North Carolina, we lived with my in-laws and I started bricklaying school in Roanoke Rapids. It didn't take me long to find out that we were not learning anything, but just wasting time.

Securing Land to Build a House
The old Oak Grove School had been put up for sale just before my discharge. I got my father-in-law to bid on it for me. The bid went to $1,000 before everyone else stopped bidding and I got the school for that price.

Re-Enlisting
In March 1954, I decided that there was not going to be any jobs available so I re-enlisted in the army where again I was sent to Fort Jackson, South Carolina to be reassigned. This time, I was given a choice of Fort Gordon, Georgia or Fort McClellan, Alabama. When told this, I remarked that this "was not much of a choice, but if I had to take one, I would rather go to Alabama."

In April 1954 I arrived at Fort McClellan. I immediately started to look for a place to stay and found a room in Montgomery.

In May 1954, my wife's Aunt Miller died and I came home for the funeral, which was handled by Cofield's Funeral Home in Weldon. While there, I picked up my wife and son to take them back to Alabama with me. After the funeral, we proceeded back to Alabama.

On the way, I found out that this was not north of the Mason Dixie line. Whenever I needed gas, I started to stop when my tank was a little less than half full. I did this because each time I stopped, I would ask the attendant for the use of his restroom, and if he said he did not have one or it was out of order, I did not buy his gas and continued on until we found a gas station that would let us use the restroom.

By the time we reached Fort McClellan, I decided that the South was not for me and immediately asked for a transfer back to Fort Dix, New Jersey.

When we reached the Georgia and Alabama state line, the speed limit changed from sixty to fifty miles per hour. We were not familiar with the laws in Alabama and did not know that the speed limit changed from sixty to fifty at night when your car lights shinned on the speed signs. We were stopped by a state trooper for going ten miles over the speed limit. Alabama was a dry state and I had just purchased a case of beer so I had my wife hide this under her feet.

The trooper explained the law concerning the changing the speed limit from day to night Although we were new in Alabama, he still gave me a ticket. I had to pay a fine and cost of court. The ticket was sent back to North Carolina where I had received a prior ticket. Within a few weeks, my mother-in-law sent me a letter from the Department of Motor Vehicle that my license had been revoked and to send them in. At that time, the state of North Carolina required a photographic copy of the license. I went to the photo lab on post and had one of my friends make a copy but while he had them on the dryer, his supervisor discovered them and tore them up. So here I was without a license.

Living in Alabama
After being in Alabama for a while, my wife and I began to like it. She met new friends where we lived and things were separated but equal. Blacks had swimming pools, a recreation center, and parks. The recreation center and park were right there where we lived. My son, Jerry, had himself a really good time in the park.

While in Alabama we met a couple by the name of Wall that worked in the local motor pool. I never had to worry about food because he kept us well supplied with eggs, bacon, and gas until one weekend he wasted oil in one of the cars. This alerted the C.I.D.[8] who started checking on him. At the time, he had a lot of oil stashed under his house. When he learned that the C.I.D. was checking on him, he left camp, went home, and moved it. The C.I.D. did not find anything and he later asked for a transfer to Fort Gordon, Georgia and received it.

My wife and I had a wonderful time in Alabama. When I had to pull C.Q.[9], she and our son Jerry came out and stayed with me all weekend. We ate in the mess hall like everyone else and the Mess Sargent would give us chickens, turkeys, and vegetables. We never had to buy much grocery.

We had a Warrant Officer in charge named DeMottie. His wife owned a meat packing plant in Anniston, Alabama and he use to let us off in the afternoon. There was a Master Sargent there by the name of Moore. He would tell me to go to the motor pool to pick up a truck after which he would load it up with garbage and take it up the hills to trade it for moonshine. He always kept a box of Tampa Nugget cigars, which he gave out to the M.P.S.[10] on the way back so that they would not search the truck. He built a cabinet in a tent, which he kept locked. This is where he stored his moonshine. He also had a Coke ice box filled with ice where he kept his beer.

One day, after we left camp with a load of garbage, we were going up a hill on the highway when one of the cans slipped on the metal strips in the body of the truck. We had garbage all up and down the road and had to do so fast scooping to clean it up.

---

[8] C.I.D. is an acronym for the Criminal Investigation Division.

[9] Charge of Quarters required a member of the armed forces to guard the front entry of the barracks.

[10] Military Police Corp.

Transfer to Fort Dix, New Jersey
In July 1954, my request for transfer to Fort Dix, New Jersey came through. I had to drive all the way through North Carolina with a revoked license. Believe me, I did not speed nor misdrive during my travel.

After arriving in Fort Dix, New Jersey, I went down and immediately changed to a New Jersey license. Both driver's license and license plates for the car were changed, which I used until my discharge in 1957. During this time, I received a letter from the North Carolina Department of Motor Vehicles stating that I could renew my license. What they did not know is that I never turned them in. This meant that all I had to do was exchange the Jersey plates for North Carolina ones.

After arriving in Fort Dix, I was assigned to the Military School system. In the Spring of 1955, I was assigned to support summer training in Fort Drum, New York. After returning back to Fort Dix, it was discovered they had too many Black Non-Commission Officers on post and had to transfer them to Fort Devens, Massachusetts.

Also, in Spring 1955, my wife and son returned back to North Carolina and we welcomed a new baby girl to the family. She told my son that, as a big brother, he would have to teach her everything he knew. When we brought our daughter home and placed her in the crib, my son ran over with a book, propped it up in front of her, and said "now let's get started." Years later we would laugh that this early beginning was how she became so smart.

Transfer to Fort Devens, Massachusetts
I arrived in Fort Devens on Columbus Day 1955 and it snowed that night. I immediately started looking for a place to live in order for my family to join me. I finally found an apartment in Leominster, Massachusetts and when we were

let off for the Christmas holidays, I proceeded home to pick up my family. The day I left camp, it was below zero degrees. Everyone had trouble getting their car started but me, even those with 1955 Mercury's.

I purchased a case of Ballentine beer and, to my surprise, it was frozen on the day I left. I proceeded to New York and stopped by my sister, Katherine, who accompanied me on the journey home. We were down in Pennsylvania before the car finally warmed up.

I spent Christmas 1955 with my in-laws and afterwards, my wife and I along with my son Jerry and daughter Debbie left for Massachusetts. This was the first time that I had all of my family with me and life was good.

Gladys in Massachusetts

Living in Massachusetts
After I got my apartment, I furnished it with furniture from Sears and Christmas 1956 was the first time my family and I spent the holidays away from home. Believe me, that was the most joyful Christmas we have ever had except for the one in which we moved into our new home that we later built in North Carolina.

On Saturday mornings, I would go to the grocery store for my family. Jerry would always stay at home with my wife and watch the funnies on TV, but Debbie made sure that she went with me to get groceries. During those years, you could get a pound of ground beef, a pound of bacon, and a pound of sausage for $1.00.

Jerry and I did a lot of fishing in Massachusetts. There were lots of lakes there and we met lots of friends. Jerry used to go to the store down the street on his own and, on his way back, he would run across the neighbor's porch. This day, he was so busy playing until he went past the house and got lost. Some of the neighbors saw him and asked him where he lived. He told them and they brought him home.

When I was assigned to Fort Devens, this put me back in the Infantry. We spent a lot of time in the field, which created a problem for me because of the frost bite I received in Korea. There were nights that my feet were in such pain, that I would get up and ride up and down the road. The next day, they found me in the Dispensary.[11]

Jerry and Debbie in Massachusetts

[11] The health facility on base.

Return to North Carolina
I was discharged in March 1957 and we returned to North Carolina. The government transported my furniture back to North Carolina. The decision was made to get out of the Army because when I tried to get Jerry enrolled in kindergarten, I was told that officers' children were accepted before all others who did not have their children already enrolled there. I made up my mind then to get out of the army because I wanted my children to have the best that public school had to offer.

Just before returning to North Carolina, my father-in-law told me that if I sent him $80.00 that he would get Lonnie Vick and they would tear down the old school house on the land we had purchased earlier. When I arrived home, they had all the nails pulled out and stacked in piles according to type. I laid the foundation and began to build. All of the neighbors gave me a hand and, by the Fall, I had framed the house up.

Living as a young family in Massachusetts

Chapter 6
Achieving the Dream

The Fall of 1957, I enrolled at St. Paul's College in Lawrenceville, Virginia and was there two weeks before receiving a letter from the VA concerning my eligibility. I was forced to withdraw until the matter was addressed and continued to do carpentry work on various projects for pay. When we had nothing to do, I would work on my house.

In 1958, our youngest daughter Sheila was born and I applied for a job at the VA Hospital in Richmond, VA. Thanks to my sister Doris who was employed there as a nurse, I found out about the job and was finally called after waiting two years to hear back from them.

In 1960, President John Kennedy was elected president. This was the first time my mother, wife, and I voted in an election. The VA Hospital called on the 22nd of February 1960 and, by the end of 1960, I had finished enough of my house to move in. My wife and I stayed in our house the night before Christmas Eve. On Christmas Eve, we got my father-in-law's old mule and wagon and finished moving in with the children who had stayed with grandparents the night before.

As mentioned before, this was one of our happier times. We had company all day until up into the night. I could finally see things falling in place. Everything I had dreamt about in my family's cotton field, working with my siblings, years before had finally come true. Everything was going fine. My wife and I had enjoyed a wonderful marriage for the past 10 years now. All we had to do was work together and move forward with the kids, who we wanted to move further than what we accomplished.

I continued to work at the VA Hospital. This required that I stay nearby, not too far from my sister Doris, and come home on Friday nights for the weekend. By the time we moved into the house, Jerry and Debbie had enrolled in school. Sheila was not yet old enough to start school, so she would visit my sister Doris and her son Keith. Her cousin Keith would also come to our house and spend time with her there.

My mother and father-in-law were also very good to us. They continued to invite us to dinner on Sundays and came to visit us under the hedge tree in our front yard. I built lawn chairs for us and we enjoyed many afternoons under that tree.

In 1966 things changed. I lost my mother-in-law, but the Lord was with us. I had applied for a job at Fort Lee, Virginia and that job came through at that time. I was finally able to be at home at night with my wife and kids.

In Chicago with my sister Doris (left) and Debbie (right).

Chapter 7
Working at Fort Lee, Virginia

When I left the VA for Fort Lee, I was told that the post was run like a dictatorship. It was later that I found this to be true.

I learned that before jobs became vacant, especially supervisory jobs, that they would place someone in the job on an interim basis and when that job was advertised, the person in the job would get it because they used experience as the main factor for qualification. The next thing I experienced was that outstanding performance and monetary awards were only given to whites.

In 1972, all whites in my section were given monetary awards. Most of them did not deserve them. One of them stated that if he could give me his, he would because he knew that he did not deserve it.

After some time, I was given a Certificate of Achievement. When I complained to the supervisor, I was told, "Since you had so much to say, you would never get one." This meant that I would never receive an award and was all I wanted to hear. I was off to the EEO Officer.

I presented a complaint to the EEO Officer who called my supervisor and asked him to come over. After a lengthy conversation, the supervisor was asked to put me back in for a Sustained Superior Award in six months.

Before the six months were up, the supervisor transferred my pay status to Enlisted Supply. When the six months were up, I went in and reminded him that it was time to put me back in for the Sustained Superior Award. To my surprise, he stated that he could not because I was not on his payroll.

He shared then that my pay had been moved to the Enlisted Supply Division.

I got permission to go to the Enlisted Supply department. There I was told that I did not work for him, that I was there only for pay purposes. He stated that he did not even know me. Upon hearing this, I immediately returned to the EEO office and again the EEO Officer called my supervisor. The Officer asked my supervisor why he had not entered the paperwork for the Sustained Superior Award. The only thing the supervisor said was that he did not have time. The EEO Officer said that was "No excuse" and that since he had "time to write the paperwork for the four white males in the section" he asked the supervisor to "go back and resubmit" my award, which he did. I finally received a monetary award in the amount of $350.00.

I was now beginning to find out what Fort Lee was all about. Because of what I encountered, I requested a transfer, but the supervisor was determined not to let me go. He did not want me to leave because that would only leave two people under his supervision.

Meanwhile, I took typing through one of the U.S. Army schools. At the end, I was told by my supervisor that the only way I could be given credit was to type 65 words per minute. I was sent over to the Personnel Office in Petersburg, which did not have anything to do with Fort Lee. When I arrived, I was given a typewriter and was told to type and given time to warm-up. The person giving the test then took the warm-up exercise and held on to it. I was then asked to start and after typing for the record, I submitted the paper only to be told that I had failed. What he had done was switched the record submission for the warm-up exercise. I learned that this was why the supervisor had sent me over to Petersburg with one of his buddies so that he could make sure that I did not pass and would have to remain in his section. After this, the division moved all the way down to the end of the post.

The day Martin Luther King was killed (April 4, 1968), my supervisor stated that this was getting serious. He left the section to hustle ammo. He got ammunition from the C.I.D. Rifle Range and Ammunition Depot. When he returned to the section, he was driving a 1964 station wagon. It was so loaded with ammunition that the rear of the car was almost touching the ground. He had a locker in the Issue Room where he stored the ammunition given to him by the C.I.D., but all he had on his station wagon was taken off post.

I knew of the ammunition in his locker, so I told my buddy to call the military police. They wanted to know who was calling. He told them it was none of their business, just do their job.

The next morning, I came in and knew where he kept the key to his locker. When I opened it, to my surprise, all the ammunition had been removed. When he would get ammunition from his friends in C.I.D., he would always give the African Americans some to take home. I still have that ammunition today as evidence.

The stress that all this caused finally began to take its toll and I spent a month at the VA Hospital in 1972. While there, I applied for a course in Radio and TV Repair under the G.I. Bill.

When I came back to work, I was determined to get out from under the supervisor. In the morning, someone from the section had to pick up the truck. Mostly this detail fell to me. One morning, I asked him why didn't "all of us have to pick up the truck." He stated that "nobody broke their backs around here" so I "shouldn't mind picking up the truck." This was the breaking point. Only the two of us were there so I backed him up against a work bench and told him this was it. I grabbed the phone and called the major at EEO and he gave me an appointment. He told me to come on over.

The Major was a Mason as well as all officers who graduated from Virginia State University. When I arrived at the EEO office, he had one of his staff members sit down with me. They went through my file to see if I qualified for any job. Meanwhile, I had my Residential Wiring License. I also had been a carpenter during the two years I waited for the job to come through after being discharged from the army. His assistant came up with a job in maintenance at Post Engineers. The very next day, I was to report for an interview. Two days later, I was on my way to a promotion from WG-6 to WG-9.

In the interim, my former supervisor was really shaken up when he heard the news. He did not know what had happened at EEO. So, I received one of the highest awards Quartermaster School Testimony. This award was the only one given.

Post Engineering
When I arrived at Post Engineers, I found I had jumped out of the frying pan into the fire. Here you found a lot of uneducated whites that came to work fighting. Most had wives who had taken advantage of them and so they took it out on everyone else. They were divorced and their ex-wives had taken their houses and money. These were some evil people at work and I was only there for a short time before I was back at the EEO.

I explained to the Officer that this was not a place I wanted to spend the rest of my time before retiring. The EEO Officer asked me how I was coming along with my studies in TV Repair. I told him that my certificate was "almost finished." He asked me to place all the courses I had completed in my life, which was placed in my file. I completed most of my courses while sitting in a maintenance truck. After I had been in Engineering about a year, a job came open in the Post Signal Audiovisual Support Center (AVSC) for an Electronics Equipment Repairer. By having put in all the courses I had taken in my records, I was more qualified than anyone else at the time.

I had been told that the supervisor of AVSC had been asking the whites to apply for the job. I reported this to the EEO Officer. He told me to go ahead and apply for the position, which I did. I was interviewed for the position and got it. This allowed me to be promoted. I had gone from a WG-6 to WG-9 to WG-10 in one year. I was learning fast how to beat the odds at Fort Lee, but it was just the beginning for a rough road that lay ahead, in front of me.

Audio-Visual Support Center
I reported to Audio-Visual to learn that African Americans had a hard time there, but I had made up my mind this was going to be my final destination until retirement.

My maintenance shop was across from the supervisor's office. The supervisor created a new position for a white employee as a GS-7 instructor for Audio-Visual. The employee learned that my position was at a higher paying job than his. All paychecks came through the office at the time and when he saw what I was getting, the supervisor immediately combined the employee's job to Wage Grade Leader WL-10 and placed him behind the desk as his assistant. The supervisor was planning to retire soon. This way, the employee would already be in the position.

I applied for the supervisor's job once it became available because I was more qualified for it. By that time, I had completed certification in Radio TV Repair school and was already in maintenance. After the interview, the white employee was given the job. I immediately filed a complaint.

The supervisor went home to take his sick leave before retiring and left the white employee in his place. That left his WL-10 open so I took this position temporarily. Meanwhile, the African Americans at Fort Lee had grown tired of their treatment on post, including systematic denial to positions for which they were more qualified and decided to do something about it.

Top: *With My Mom and Sister Esther*

Bottom: *With My Sister Katherine*

Chapter 8
Activism for Civil Rights

There was a gentleman from Richmond named Emory Rueben Green who was spearheading a discrimination complaint against Fort Lee. The only thing he had to do was find enough name plaintiffs in order to get the suit off the ground. In 1979, he finally got enough people willing to step forward. Including Emory R. Green and myself, those brave enough to come forward included Joyce Massenburg, Shirley Dexter, Shirley Mitchell, Patricia Morgan, Willie Munford (Jr.), Sue Richardson, Theodore C. Richardson, Rosa White, Gladorin G. Williams, Willie P. Brown, Melvin B. Evans, and Oscar L. Flowkes. All others on base who were African Americans in similar situations were afraid of losing their jobs.

The suit was served on the General at Fort Lee by Federal Marshalls. When everyone on base found out about it, most thought we were crazy and that all of us would be fired. They soon discovered that we were not insane and had been successful in addressing the issue of discrimination on base. When the Consent Decree was approved by Judge Warner of Richmond, African Americans who were reluctant on base started to sign up along with us for the monetary compensation awarded. The Consent Decree, which addressed what was required for Fort Lee was approved for a period of three years.

Attorney Marsh who represented those of us who were among the eleven plaintiffs in the case made up a final distribution of the monetary compensation each person was to receive along with other benefits. After receiving a copy, I was notified that I was to name my career goal and would receive training towards that goal. However, no monetary compensation was attached.

Once the distribution list was completed, we all met in court before Judge Warner at which time I reminded him that I had been discriminated against and told him the page and paragraph he would find references to my case. The judge stated that he knew I was telling the truth because he had a copy of the complaint and then asked Attorney Marsh what he intended to do about compensation. Marsh stated that he would give me money. The judge informed Attorney Marsh that he did not see this in the paperwork submitted and asked him to take it back and read it. The paperwork was corrected and re-submitted.

When the dust settled, I received the second largest amount awarded in the case. This was because the Judge decided that the eleven named plaintiffs should receive the bulk of the money awarded and stated that this was because he knew what we had gone through in order to get the complaint before the court.

Road to Becoming Audio-Visual Director
As required by the Court Decree, my supervisor and I met with Civilian Personnel to discuss my career goal. At the meeting, I stated that my goal was to become Audio-Visual Director. When I stated this, the staffer asked my supervisor, "That's your job isn't it?" The supervisor agreed that this was, and then, when assigning my training for the job, recommended a correspondence course that would take over a year to complete. He then stated he was retiring and assigned the white employee to his position while he used up his remaining sick leave. He did this knowing I would not be qualified in time before his official retirement date given that the course would not be completed until afterwards. He clearly wanted to shift the outcome to favor the white employee by giving him the interim role for the position.

After the meeting, I met with Rueben Green who spearheaded the lawsuit against Fort Lee and told him what happened.

He advised me to enroll at Virginia State University and apply for all the courses that would qualify me for the job, which I did.

As soon as I enrolled, the supervisor stated that the courses did not pertain to the job. The courses were Elementary Writing, Advanced Communication Skills, Educational TV, and the Selection and Utilization of Media. I continued to take these courses. The Major over the manager then informed me that I would get a new training schedule and that the supervisor was not going to make it.

I received a new training schedule that provided preparation in all areas of leadership as an Audio-Visual Director. I went to school in Richmond, Fort Lee, and Norfolk in Virginia and in Philadelphia, PA. My attorney stated "This time, no one can say that you are not qualified for the job." He added, "The only thing, they can say now is that you are over qualified."

I also received a course in Evaluations of Employees and learned about the class despite efforts in the office to stop me from knowing it would be offered. A driver who had brought in our distribution noticed the course posted on the bulletin board and explained to me what it was all about. However, when I went to review the posting, it had been removed. Thanks to the driver, I knew that the class was posted because he had told me it was there and what was included in the course description. I therefore went into the office and asked my supervisor where the posting was that explained what the course was about. He looked in the trash can and there it was. The assistant who was going to take his place had removed the posting, torn it up, and put it in the trash. I took tape and put it back together for this was exactly what I was going to write-up for qualification purposes.

The next problem I had was qualification in Supply Training. I was told by my supervisor that the training would last sixteen weeks. I immediately went to the Major and he changed it to two weeks and completed the training along with other officers on base. By now, everything I did was really getting next to the white supervisor and co-worker because they could not stop me from qualifying for the job. They knew that, with this training, I would also qualify as a Supply Officer.

The supervisor finally left the office to use up his sick leave. While he was gone, I took courses in Security and Budgeting at Fort Lee and Personnel Administration at Virginia State.

While the supervisor was on leave, the Colonel caught him over town directing traffic and made him come back to work. This really threw a monkey-wrench in the assistant's interim position. Once the supervisor was back, the assistant now had to figure out another way to out-qualify me.

Application for the Audio-Visual Services Officer Position
In 1983, the supervisor finally retired for good. As soon as he did, the assistant took over the office given that he had served in the interim role previously.

To out-qualify me for the position, the assistant decided to combine Supply Officer along with Audio-Visual Service's Officer and come up with the title Supply and Audiovisual Services Officer. His thinking was that he would combine the two jobs and, since he would be serving in both positions, that he would out-qualify me. Before he could complete the revised position description, the job for Audio-Visual Services Officer was advertised. However, the announcement was never posted on the office bulletin board so that I could not find out about the position available.

The day before the time for all personnel were to apply for the job, one of my carpool riders who worked in the mail room happened to see the posting and called me about it. I immediately went to see the assistant who was now acting as my supervisor and he finally gave me a copy.

The advertisement was to expire on Monday and here it was the Friday before. That meant that I had to prepare a résumé by the Monday deadline. I worked all weekend to do so and got my niece to type while I wrote it up on paper. We finished the résumé at 9:00pm Sunday night, but it was ready for submission on Monday morning.

On Monday, I took the résumé to the EEO and left a copy. By this time, all of my training had been completed and documented in office files. All I had to do now was wait for my interview.

Interview, Outcome, and Overcoming New Barriers to Success
When we finally received word about the date of the interview, I was prepared. My children were in college at the time and had advised me on how to dress for a supervisor's job and I dressed accordingly.

The interview panel consisted of one African American, one Chinese, and the five whites. The one African American panelist later told me that I had answered the questions "far superior" to that of the white employee.

In addition to the interview, I was asked to take a test.

I later discovered that the former supervisor had made up the test taken to fit the assistant's specific on-the-job training. He received the job.

Although the white employee had been the assistant and left in the job by my former supervisor during his sick leave, I had actually learned the job by answering the phone while he and the supervisor were out drinking during the day. They would leave me in the office each morning, come back at lunch to see what was happening, and then leave again. This was a daily routine with them.

My repair shop was across from the office, so when the phone rang, I answered it and, in the process, received training specific to the job. I got it because no one else was there. A secretary was later hired to fill the job a former secretary held.

I was not notified in the office who had received the position. When this occurred, I went to EEO and it was then that I was told that the white employee had gotten the job. I was also informed that, if I intended to file a complaint, I must do so right away and I did.

The white employee was really surprised by the new complaint. He knew that if the time had expired for me to file this that he would have been home free in securing the position. As a result of the complaint, I was placed in his former assistant's job, which was WL-10 Leader. This was supposed to satisfy me, but to his surprise, I challenged the decision for the job desired.

Meanwhile, the white employee had taken the position and completed an official inventory of equipment, which he indicated totaled one and a half million dollars.

After filing the complaint, I went to the Personnel Office to check my records on file only to be told that I could not. This happened even though I had just been there to see the records two days before. I knew then something was fishy and went to look at the bulletin board. It was then that I saw a notice that the Consent Decree was going to expire the next day.

I immediately called Attorney James R. Walker who advised me to come over when I got home and to bring a copy of the Consent Decree with me. The next morning, he studied the Decree and by 10:00am, looked up at me and stated "I got them." He had found where Fort Lee had violated 3E and 4A of the Consent Decree, which stated:

It shall be the policy and practice of the defendants not to discriminate against any employee because of race in its personnel decisions, details, assignment of duties, training opportunities, appraisals, awards, and disciplinary actions, to include promotion and de-assignment to middle and upper grade position, including supervisory positions, at Fort Lee.

It was after 4:00 pm when we finally finished putting a motion together to have the Consent Decree extended because Fort Lee was not in compliance and had violated it by using an unauthorized test, which was not approved by the EEOC. The supervising manager had used a test that he thought only favored the white employee.

I left Weldon where Attorney Walker lived and headed for Richmond at approximately 3:40 pm. I arrived at the courthouse in Richmond ten minutes to 5:00 pm, just in time to get the motion filed.

The next day, one of the employees who was a named plaintiff in the case went to EEOC and told the EEO Officer that I had filed a motion to have the Consent Decree extended. The EEO Officer told her that this would "not do any good" because "Fort Lee filed a motion to have the Consent Decree ended three days ago." How wrong this proved to be.

After Judge Warner studied what had occurred in my case, he filed an order extending the Consent Decree "indefinitely" as to the parties of Wright, White, and Dexter. This happened solely because what that had occurred with us on or before the cut-off date of the earlier decree.

Back on the Road to Achieving Career Goal

The next day, the EEO officer had been transferred so she would not be available to be questioned. The following day, I received notice that I had been promoted to Audio-Visual Services Officer. However, I was to "remain in my same position until such time the new position became vacant." The white assistant would therefore remain in the supervisor's position.

I received a rate increase on February 7, 1983. However, I did not receive a promotion because they back-dated this to the one previously described, which was received after the Consent Decree was extended and had occurred before February 7, 1983. I ended up getting less money than I would have received had I stayed in my former job. This occurred to keep me from receiving more pay than the white employee who was already in the job. The situation did not leave me with anything to do so I used up a lot of my excess sick leave for the rest of the year.

In the summer of 1983, the white employee increased his salary by combining the Audio-Visual with Supply, which he completed after the former Supply Officer retired.

On December 1, 1983, the C.I.D. began to find televisions, cassette players, and projectors in units of Fort Lee that was not on anyone's Hand Receipt. This continued and was later reported to the General.

The General set up a team to conduct a physical inventory of all equipment assigned to Fort Lee. The team took over our office and the supervisor disappeared. He knew that he was now in a lot of trouble. The team concluded that he had taken over two sections without inventorying any equipment.

By Christmas, the team had found thousands of dollars of missing equipment. In the Supply Section alone that the supervisor had taken over, the team discovered hand receipts that had not been updated in seven years, which should have been done every six months. The former supervisor and assistant who was now in charge were alcoholics. These people came to work just to get paid and could get away with it because all highly paid and supervisory jobs where held by whites.

In January 1984 alone, the team found over a thousand dollars of equipment at Fort Picket that was not accounted for. By the first of March 1984, the Captain in charge of the inventory met with the General to make his report. This was the General's breaking point. He ordered the Captain to report back and asked that the manager and supervisor be fired immediately. He also requested that Rueben Green, who had spearheaded the suit against Fort Lee, be placed in the manager's job. After Mr. Green was placed in the manager's job, he asked if I would take the position as head of Audio Visual Services, which I agreed. The white employee assigned as supervisor did not have enough time to retire and was assigned to Supply as a truck driver in which he remained until his eligibility for retirement.

Life as Audio-Visual Chief
After taking over the Audio-Visual Center, the Signal building where we were housed previously came up for renovation. The Photo Lab and Audio-Visual Center were removed from the building. The Photo Lab was placed in trailers and Audio-Visual Support was placed in a warehouse at the end of the post, away from everything. When the renovation completed, the Photo Lab returned back to the Signal building while I remained in a warehouse. This brought about

another complaint of discrimination in building assignment given that the Signal building was designed especially for the Audio-Visual Support Center. There was a classroom for training personnel from various organizations on the proper way to operate the equipment issued by Fort Lee. We also had projection booths to preview films, and an Issue Room to issue equipment along with a Film Issue and Repair Room. We also had double offices—one for the head of Audio-Visual and one for the secretary who also worked with supply records.

I won the new complaint in August of 1988. Fort Lee also agreed that I was suitable for the Audio-Visual assignment. As a result of the complaint, they further agreed that African Americans would no longer be discriminated against when assessing the pay-grade level for supervisory positions. For this work, I was given an Exceptional Performance Award.

As a result of the complaint's outcome, discriminatory acts no longer allowable at Fort Lee included the following: (1) excluding African American supervisors in the chain-of-command, (2) assignment to inferior work sites to African Americans, (3) failure to give work assistance needed to African American supervisors, (4) excluding African Americans when issuing awards, (5) compromising complaints from African Americans by requiring them to do acts and perform tasks not required of white supervisors, and (6) discriminating due to retirement age and prior service.

I thought that this would be my last and final complaint, but I there was still one left.

Final Victory in Addressing Discrimination
The last complaint filed was Fort Lee's failure to correct my salary to reflect the promotion. I could have retired a year earlier. However, I was waiting for the court to rule on a complaint previously filed. Meanwhile, things at Fort Lee

were still far from being acceptable, but African Americans had come a long way. They were now managers, supervisors, and many had been given awards, including monetary awards.

In January 1988 I attended a supervisor's meeting. The General told all supervisors that there would be "no more discrimination at Fort Lee." He stated that, "if African Americans and whites were equally qualified for a job, that the job would be given to the African American" because "they were still underrepresented in the workforce." He also stated that "any supervisor had a complaint coming to them and failed to correct it" and "they went off-post" that the supervisor would be "sent out the gate."

As soon as the General left, the white supervisors stated "the General wasn't going to tell them who to hire" and that they were "going to hire who [they] wanted to." This was ten years after the discrimination complaint was filed against Fort Lee.

Attorneys from Virginia looked down on me because I was from North Carolina and did not try to help me, but thanks to Attorney James R. Walker, Jr. from Weldon, we were able to out maneuver the government lawyers. We challenged them in every area of the workforce and were consistently successful.

In March 1989, I retired from Fort Lee, but there was still one more battle and that was my salary had not been corrected. The day I retired another white person had retired with me. She had been on sick leave for the entire year. All she had to do was pick up her check on payday.

Once I retired, I got in touch with Congressman Jones and asked him to get my pay records. I told him I thought that Fort Lee had either altered or destroyed my pay records.

When he asked them for this, Fort Lee informed him that the records had already been sent off post. He told me not to worry, that they would get them. After being given the run around, the records finally arrived. It was then that I discovered that the pay records had been altered to reflect that I was compensated appropriately back in 1983. The one who was responsible for this had been made to retire. All I wanted was for Fort Lee to make the correction and provide appropriate compensation for my work.

After my congressman received the records, I began to correspond with Fort Lee. They told my congressman that my pay had already gone to court and that therefore they did not owe me anything. I let them know that the promotion had been awarded before the court decision, but that pay had not.

In October 1989, I went to the Council of Deliberation meeting in Charlotte. On the way back, I stopped by to see Attorney Walker. By now, he was completely blind, but he remembered the complaint. He told me to stick to one thing—that I was not given a hearing therefore my complaint had not gone to court and that they were in violation of my fifth amendment to the United States Constitution. I maintained this argument until the case was finally resolved in 1998.

A copy of all of my correspondence was sent to President Clinton, Attorney General Reno, Secretary of the Army Togo West, Congressman Eva Clayton, Mrs. Mary L. Peeler (then Executive Director of the NAACP), Revered Curtis Harris as President of the Virginia chapter of the Southern Christian Leadership Conference (SCLC), Gilbert F. Cossellas EEOC, Mrs. Doris Cochran as Executive Secretary of the Eastern Council on Community Affairs, and Mr. Rueben Green, my former manager.

My complaint was sent off post twice during this time, but I did not let this phase me. I would continue to write until it was sent back to Fort Lee. The last time my complaint was sent off post to the Compliance and Complaints Review Agency of the Department of the Army on Jefferson Davis Highway, in Arlington, Virginia. This time, Attorney Walker advised me to file a new complaint, this way they could not claim this was an old complaint. It took two letters before they got the picture and finally accepted my complaint. The Department called the EEO Officer at Fort Lee, but they failed to answer the phone. However, they sent a letter to the Post Commander requesting that the matter be settled.

It was not until the 15th of October, 1997 that I met with the in EEO. One of the girls in the EEO stated that she would "like to see this Henry Wright" because of the many letters she received from 1989 to now concerning "this same matter." One of the old employees told her this was "nothing new" because she "had to put up with Mr. Wright many years while he was employed there."

Mr. Emory (Rueben) Green was still employed at Fort Lee and represented me in the complaint. In January, I was finally compensated. However, my monthly paycheck is still short by $200.

Chapter 9
Final Thoughts

I am writing this to show the discrimination I went through during federal employment. It took many hours, many nights, and I was unable to sleep. Many letters and many motions were filed with the federal court. When I retired in 1989 and finally came to an agreement during the final complaint, I resigned from the fight in discrimination. My wife used to ask me, "Why does it always have to be you?" I told her, "If not me, who?" and that I had made a promise to my 24th Infantry Regiment comrades that I would do as much as I could after the Korean War in the fight for Civil Rights. I have truly kept that promise and feel that God kept me through the war for some reason. God always has someone to fight who is willing to put his life on the line for what he believes in.

Similar Dynamics within the Community
While fighting for our civil rights with the government, I had to also fight for civil rights at my church. I had worked with SCLC in Virginia along with Reverend Curtis Harris, but I was also Recording Secretary for the NAACP in North Carolina.

In 1866, right after the Civil War ended, some of my forefathers needed to build a church so they purchased 50 acres from the family of Nancy Kee. There was 14 acres open and was continued to be cultivated my Mrs. Kee until her death. The whole 50 acres would become property of Roanoke Salem Baptist Church. After her death, the church continued to let whites farm the land in order to keep the weeds down. Each time our forefathers would confront them, the white farmers would tell them that they did not "need all that land."

In 1975, I became a trustee of the Roanoke Salem Baptist Church. The issue of the land came up again after the church started to cut trees down on the property for a parking lot. Dr. C. L. Sykes had been tending the 14 open acres of land formerly kept by Ms. Kee for this purpose and had decided that this was his, so he filed a motion for a restraining order in court to keep the church from cutting timber on the land. There were 8 trustees being sued and I was one of them. I was also appointed secretary of the board.

In 1975, the Church hired Weldon Attorney James R. Walker to defend the land.

On April 27, 1981, a hearing was held at the Court House and later moved to the Public Library where deacons Jacob Rice and I were forced to become spokesmen for the trustees after Judge Nicholas Long denied Attorney Walker the right to defend his clients by claiming that he did not have a license to practice law. However, Walker knew that they were going to do this and had discussed it with us. He asked the two of us to place the matter before the court ourselves and call him as a witness. That way, he could get everything he wanted to on the record. At the end, we appealed the case to Raleigh in order to get it out of the racist hands of the locals. We finally were able to get the case heard.

In 1991, the money in Escrow was returned to the church, thus ending the fight to secure boundaries to land that had belonged to the church for the past 127 years.

Postscript

It is here that my father ends his story. Yet, it is not the whole story and I must add my own perspectives. When my parents got married, my father said "I do" and my mother reportedly said "I will try." They must have tried really hard. My parents were married over 50 years before my mother lost a fearless battle with cancer. She left the planet in 2001 on an early Christmas morning. Somehow, she talked her doctors into letting her come home. My father, the Buffalo Soldier who had fought in Korea at the Battle of Chosin Reservoir told us afterwards that following behind mom's ambulance that day was "the hardest thing I ever had to do." The man who built the house where we lived out of recycled wood from my mother's one-room school house and to whom everyone would ask for help repairing VCRs, TVs, and just about everything electrical—the man who probably should have been an electrical engineer—would now say "it was the one thing he could not fix."

Luckily, on their 50th anniversary, my parents finally got the honeymoon they never received before my father went to Korea. Thanks to the generosity of my sister, they went to Hawaii and loved it. My sister and I went with them and witnessed a transformation for both. Looking out at the sunset, they reminisced and commented how my grandparents (her mother and father) would have loved seeing them. After my mom's departure, Daddy – the one who wanted to see the world and ended up in Korea instead – began to travel. Mostly he traveled with my sister – occasionally taking a break to explore on his own. When traveling by himself, my sister was always concerned that he would forget where he was. When asked about his whereabouts, Daddy always says "if I can get in and out of Korea, I can get in and out of [fill in the blank.]" It is wonderful that he has finally seen the world and has traveled to many places, including Italy, France, Spain, the UK, Greece, and Israel. He always wanted my mother to see Korea, but she never did and he's never been back.

On Memorial Day of each year Daddy is always asked to speak somewhere within his local community. This past year, he received an award for his service and we all cheered. Daddy also regularly visits local schools to talk with children about Buffalo Soldiers. Each year he travels to a national conference to be with other Buffalo Soldiers. Now 88, he says this year might be his last time. Traveling gets more difficult with each passing year. Truth is, many of his friends are no longer here.

Once, I asked my father what is the most difficult part of growing old. His answer was seeing the erosion of humanity. I also once asked him the most important thing to remember. His answer was "to protect education at all costs." An advocate for human and civil rights, he also once told me it was important to always remember to "never become the thing you fight." Education is important to my father. He still has his grades from the first term of college on his wall and is especially proud of the fact that he educated his children. His son, my brother Jerry, is a poet and writer who lived in New York for years and has now returned home. He briefly lived in the very house where he first grew up – my grandparent's house – before owning his own after the land was taken for a new superhighway to the beach; he now lives near where he went to high school.

My sister Debbie and I live in Chicago. In the 1970s Debbie was the first Valedictorian of first-generation African descent from her high school. Like Daddy, she loved math and science. She went to medical school, then law school, and became a prominent patent attorney with large corporations and bar associations. She is now retired and busily engaged in the arts and on a number of other boards, including social organizations and the Ryan Opera Center for the Lyric Opera of Chicago.

Me, I am the youngest daughter who learned a lot from her father. An artist by training, I met and married my husband shortly after saying goodbye to Mom. We were married in Maui – the same place that my parents had gone on their 50th Anniversary. Unbeknown to him at the time, the violinist my husband hired to play at our wedding turned out to be the same one who played in the background while my sister and I dined with my parents one evening in Maui. Curious, my parents asked at that time why Debbie and I had not married. Flippantly, I said "the only way I would get married is if I had a house over here and he had a house over there." Shortly after, Richard and I were married and, just like Mom and Dad, were inseparable. A professor, I chose a path in administration, which eventually led to four years of traveling back and forth between Boston and Chicago. I am now back in Chicago full-time where, like my father, I still passionately champion equity and inclusive practices in the arts and education. A humanitarian who enjoys giving back, I decided to publish Daddy's story in his own words so that all would know that Henry finally saw the world, is a Buffalo Soldier of distinction, a devoted husband, and loving Daddy of three. Happy Birthday Daddy! We love you.

Epilogue

Before she left the planet, my mother told me that I was just like my father. In asking why, she responded that we both share a relentless passion to fight for what we believe is right and to support others who experienced life similarly in our quest for justice, equity, and equality for all. We also share a love of country and desire equal access to lead a more prosperous life in our pursuit of happiness. Our human bond is further shaped by our shared talent for building things and tinkering around with images, our big hearts, and passion for all that it good in the world.

My parents taught me to stand up for what is right and that is precisely what I aspire to do. My father taught me never to become the thing that I fight and that is precisely how I live. After all, acceptance and acknowledgement of others in their quest to, as my friend Georgette Norman says, "simply be" in the world is who we are at our core.

My father and I both grew up in the midst of national change. He in the 40s and 50s, me in the 60s and 70s. What we witnessed, what we endured, and what we accomplished in spite of the odds was an astonishing test of endurance and inner strength. Our achievement to some is nothing short of a miracle and to others simply social resilience shaped by intellectual curiosity and creative efficacy. Yet, there is so much more to the story.

Our life is a testament to what it means to invest in the cultivation of our vast interior landscape and mind's eye; to have hope and vision for a better present, a more caring and loving future, and the faith to seek our highest self while being cognizant of the world around us.

As we witness the dawning years of the new millennium, it is clear that many do not share these aspirations. Yet now, as much as at any time in the past, it is time for all to recognize the age-old threats to freedom, justice and peace. To that end we would be wise to forgive past transgressions, real or imagined, to care for one another, and to recognize the strength that comes from unity within our diversity.

To do anything less dishonors those who came before us and what they taught us about taking the high road. My father would agree that we have a responsibility to become aware of those who came before us, and the personal sacrifices they made to enable us to be here today. Understanding the past allows us to put our own challenges into the proper perspective.

Finally, in the closing lines of "Middlemarch," George Eliot writes that

> " . . . the growing good of the world is partly dependent on unhistoric acts; and that things are not so ill with you and me as they might have been, is half owing to the number who lived faithfully [a life of small, unnumbered acts of caring and courage and self-sacrifice.]"

Henry, my father, would also agree with that.

Sheila Wright Stamm

www.ingramcontent.com/pod-product-compliance
Lightning Source LLC
Chambersburg PA
CBHW052117070526
44584CB00017B/2520